IMPACT OF MOTIVATION

DR. JAGADEESH PILLAI

Made with ♥ on the Notion Press Platform
www.notionpress.com

Dedicated to all those people around the world who are feeling despondent. We recognize the struggles you are facing and want to extend our support. No matter how dark the days may seem, we hope you can find solace in knowing that you are not alone. Together, we can work to create a brighter future.

Contents

Contents

Prayer

Ganga tharanga ramaneeya jata kalapam,
Gowri niranthara vibhooshitha vama bhagam,
Narayana priya mananga madapaharam,
Varanasi pura pathim Bhajha Viswanatham ||

About The Author

Dr. Jagadeesh Pillai four times Guinness World Record holder, a voracious reader, writer, and true research scholar was born in Varanasi, the abode of Lord Shiva. He is Ph.D. in Vedic Science. He is a multi-faceted polymath with innate qualities, creative ideas and many remarkable achievements. Although his roots extend back to "Gods own Country"(Kerala), the residents of Varanasi feel proud of him and adore him as a child of Varanasi who caters to every individual in need without any expectations. A deep study into his profile reflects that he has added so many feathers to his cap which makes him quite unique. He is a four times Guinness Book of World Records Holder in the following subjects :

1. "Script to Screen" which he achieved by producing and directing a state of art animation film within the shortest time possible by breaking the earlier set record by Canadians. There are many national and international Awards and Recognitions to his credit.
2. Longest Line of Post Cards which he has done on the occasion of 163 years of Indian Postal Day by 16300 post cards. The event was also connected with a questionnaire about Indian Flag.
3. Largest Poster Awareness Campaign – This was achieved by designing an awareness campaign on the subject "Beti Bachao – Beti Padhao".
4. Largest Envelop – Towards tribute to Prime Minister's initiative 'Make in India' – he has created about 4000 sq meter envelop using waste papers.
5. Attempted by lighting 70000 candles on a 210 kg cake to

celebrate the 70th Indian Independence day recorded in World Records India.

6. Attempted a documentary on Dhamek Stupa of Sarnath dubbing in 17 languages, result is waiting from Guinness World Records.

He is versatile in Gita teaching. The young generation is fond of his Gita teaching and he has changed the life of many young through his continued motivational boost up and teachings.

He has composed and sung Gayatri Mantra in 1008 different tunes.

He has composed and sung Hanuman Chalisa in 108 different tunes.

He has composed and sung hundreds of Sanskrit Bhajans, Patriotic songs, etc.

He has written and directed so many short films and documentaries for awareness campaigns.

He has done voluntary services to UP Police and Kerala Police to spread awareness campaigns on the various issue through videos and photography.

He is on the path of authoring thousands of books on Indian culture, Indian Temples, and the life of extraordinary people.

It is hard to believe that he has produced and directed more than 100 Documentaries on a particular city (Varanasi) which is done by a single person.

He has helped and guided more than 25 boys and girls

to achieve world records through various creative and innovative methods.

A multifaceted person who can apply the best of his intellect using the God-given blessings which have been showered upon every human being granting them an immense capacity to learn, experience, and experiment with many things and do wonders in this world of discrimination and disparities.

He is a teacher and a student at the same time who always learns every day and teaches every day. As a master, his weakness was that he never sticks to a particular subject. Perhaps this weakness gives him the strength to master any area which he came across.

Each of his days dawned with learning a new topic and he spend most of his time experimenting and researching it.

He is also a selfless social activist and a motivational speaker.

His life was full of struggle, ups and downs, and failures. But he never gave up and faced all his trials and tribulations full of confidence. Today he is a successful young man with a lot of enthusiasm and rich life experience.

He has sung full Ram Charita Manas 51 hours audio by his own composition. He has also sung the whole Bhagavad-Gita in his own composition with a rhythmic background.

He has also sung "Lokah Samastha Sukhino Bhavantu" in 50 different languages.

Currently working on a detailed and scientific study on Veda, Upanishad, Puranas, Bhagavad Gita, etc.

He has composed and sung Hanuman Chalisa in 108 different compositions and Gayatri Mantra in 1008 different compositions.

<u>Awards</u>

Four Times Guinness World Records

Winner of Mahatma Gandhi Vishwa Shanti Puraskar

Mahatma Gandhi Global Peace Ambassador

Kashi Ratna Award

Dr. APJ Abdul Kalam Motivational Person of the Year 2017

Mother Teresa Award

Indira Gandhi Priyadarshini Award

Bharat Vikas Ratna Award

Udyog Ratna Award

Vigyan Prasar Award

Poorvanchal Ratn Samman

Preface

No matter how much we try to wish otherwise, life is often full of struggles, moments of despondency, and inescapable disappointments. Nowhere is this truer than in our daily lives, when we try to navigate the often confusing and disheartening mix of decisions that steer our path into the future. Unforseen and unavoidable circumstances can often arise when we least expect them, leading to setbacks and failure. This often complex journey that we trudge through, while being dogged at every step by struggles, can become overwhelming and leave us feeling disheartened and despondent.

At times, it may seem as though we are powerless against the stumbling blocks that appear to thwart our best laid plans. We can never be fully prepared for some of the difficulties that come our way, or for the moment when we discover that our expectations have not been met. It can be incredibly difficult to keep going, or to find a way forward when the future seems foggy. Minor failures and disappointments can pile up one after the other, and can transform into greater problems, spiraling into a decline of our overall wellbeing.

In order to remain strong in the face of these disheartening realities, it's important to understand and remember that failure is a natural part of life. Learning to accept that not everything in life goes as we had hoped, gives us the strength and resilience to persevere when times get tough. Taking regular time to appreciate the little wins and successes we achieve, creating a positive mindset to help reframe our outlook on the more challenging times, and seeking consolation in meaningful relationships with those closest to us, are all tactics that can help us keep afloat and avoid burning-out in the face of constant strain.

Though life is sometimes challenging and filled with difficulty, we should always strive to push forward and make the most of the opportunities that come our way, even in moments of dispair. Doing so will not only help us to learn and grow from our mistakes, but will also allow us to better understand the importance of self-reflection and resilience. Struggles, despondency, and disappointments are unavoidable, but with the right mindset and attitude, we can anticipate and move forward through any situation.

Life is full of struggles, despondency, and disappointments. Proper motivation can act as a tonic to encourage those who are feeling down. My enthusiasm to explore the depths of motivation is documented in this book.

WHAT IS MOTIVATION AND HOW IT CAN CHANGE A PERSON'S ATTITUDE

Motivation is a powerful driving force within human insecurity, inspiring an individual to initiate action, persist and attain success. It is capable of unlocking a person's potential and transforming attitudes, allowing them to reach new heights they thought were unattainable. This inner force can come from various external sources such as family, friends, work, and even societal norms. Through proper harnessing, motivation can lead to improved behaviour, healthier outlooks and a better quality of life.

What motivates us to take risks, explore new possibilities, and strive for greater achievement varies from person to person. Additionally, it also changes over time due to changes in our environment and our own personal growth and transformation. Ultimately, motivation is a combination of internal and external influences that determine why we do and don't do certain things. Internally, it is made up of things like values, emotions, beliefs, and preferences. While externally, motivation is derived from external pressures and the availability of resources and rewards.

On a personal level, motivation is both an enabler and an agent of change, allowing individuals to recognize and seize opportunities, develop healthier relationships, and realize goals. It is a powerful tool that can enable one to take control and reach greater heights of success. If a person is not motivated, then the remainder of their aspirations and ambitions may never be fully achieved.

Yet, motivation isn't always easy to summon. For many, re-igniting one's inner fire can be difficult. Practicing self-awareness, developing positive coping habits, and adopting new and effective strategies and techniques can be useful aids in connecting with motivation. Once within reach, motivation provides an incredible advantage in life, allowing individuals to transform their attitudes and performance. It helps them to approach life with confidence, enthusiasm, and resilience, thereby increasing potential for success.

It is worth noting that the process of becoming motivated and changing one's attitude can take repeated effort over time. The potential rewards of such an endeavour, however, can be could not be greater. By properly harnessing internal and external motivators, individuals can reclaim the power to become agents of change and to reach heights of success and wellbeing that were once thought unattainable.

CHAPTER TWO

MOTIVATIONAL SPEECHES

Motivational speeches are an important element of personal growth and development, especially for those dealing with depression. For a depressed individual, there may be too much negative talk overwhelming them and preventing them from believing in a positive future. The aim of a motivational speech is to provide uplifting words of encouragement to empower the individual and motivate them to achieve their potential.

A motivational speech must be tailored to the individual's specific needs, focusing on life experiences, building self-esteem, breaking negative thought patterns, and inspiring hope for the future. The speaker should take the time to research the individual's history, future prospects, and current situation as deeply as possible to ensure the inspirational words are tailored accurately. It is important to affirm the individual's potential, instil hope, build courage and self-belief, and provide useful strategies to prevent them from falling back into a depressive state. A few minutes of motivational support can make all the difference in the world.

Motivational speeches can provide a sense of meaning and purpose to those dealing with debilitating depression. The person is presented with practical ideas and strategies to make positive changes in their life and to move forward in changing circumstances. The individual is encouraged to make the positive life changes they need to create a brighter future and to stay motivated until they reach success.

In addition, motivational speeches can help to empower individuals by recognizing their challenges and providing them with the confidence to make desired changes. Through a motivational speech, individuals can appreciate their strengths, recognize the areas where they lack self-confidence, and take control of their own lives. The purpose is to encourage the individual to take practical steps towards the realization of their aims and to live life to the fullest.

Overall, motivational speeches have the potential to create a life-changing impact among those dealing with depression. This type of speech is integral to the personal development of individuals and provides them with the courage and support they need to erase self-doubt, break negative thought patterns, unlock their potentials, and live a life of meaning and purpose. Utilizing the power of inspirational words, motivational speeches can encourage individuals to make positive changes in their lives and take control of their own destinies.

CHAPTER THREE

MOTIVATIONAL SPEAKERS

Motivational speakers have become a very important part of our society, as they attempt to inspire people to reach their goals. They help people to tap into their inner power and push themselves to do better by motivating them to get out of their comfort zone and take risks in order to find success. Motivational speakers share their knowledge, stories and experiences to motivate, inspire and empower those that relate to their story.

Thoughts and attitude of motivational speakers vary based on the individual and the message they are trying to convey. Generally, motivational speakers talk from a positive viewpoint and promote personal responsibility as a key to succeeding in life. They may encourage people to focus on the solutions and stop dwelling on the negative. Motivational speakers also attempt to instil an abundant mindset, that there are unlimited possibilities and resources out there to achieve our goals. They will often emphasize on the importance of having a growth mindset and a determination to not give up.

Motivational speakers also provide encouragement and affirmation. They understand the importance of momentum. They provide the push for us to move toward our goals, often interlacing stories of their own successes and failures to provide more understanding of the topic at hand. They draw from their own experiences and those of other successful people to inspire their audience.

Motivational speakers also promote personal development by focusing on the importance of self-awareness, setting goals and taking action. They talk about setting intentions, discovering and developing our strengths, being true to our values, and developing a positive mindset. They also focus on the power of systematizing processes, delegating tasks and setting deadlines as a way to improve and take going farther.

The thoughts and attitude of motivational speakers has a direct effect on their audiences. Through the transmission of positive messages and motivational stories, they help to motivate and shift people's mind-sets, empowering the people in their audience and helping them to reach their goals. The visual and auditory cues of motivational speakers signifying their enthusiasm, commitment and passion help to draw in the listeners and engage them in the message being conveyed.

In conclusion, motivational speakers have a strong influence on their audiences by promoting a positive attitude and inspiring people to reach their goals. They emphasize personal responsibility and drive home the message that we are the masters of our own destiny. They share their own experiences to motivate and inspire their listeners and help them reach their personal best.

CHAPTER FOUR

IMPACT OF MOTIVATIONAL QUOTES

It is no secret that motivational quotes can have a huge impact on how people live, think, and achieve their goals. Motivational quotes can act as a source of inspiration, helping to provide an uplifting and inspiring outlook on life. Many people look to the words of others for comfort, understanding, and guidance, ultimately having a profound influence on their decisions and actions.

Motivational quotes can have a positive effect on a person's outlook and attitude. This is because the quotes can provide individuals with a sense of structure and direction, making them feel more confident and in control of their lives. Moreover, these quotes can help to provide clarity, with some being able to bring an individual to a place of contemplation and introspection. As a result, people can feel a sense of self-awareness and understanding, as well as feeling more driven and motivated to achieve their goals.

Motivational quotes can also be effective in encouraging personal growth. This is because they provide a means of tracking progress and personal development. Individuals can be reminded of the progress they have already made and can look to the uplifting words of others to provide the necessary impetus to keep going. By being surrounded by progressive messages, individuals can remain motivated and gain the confidence and guidance to move closer to achieving their goals.

It is not just individuals who can benefit from motivational quotes. Companies and organizations can also utilize quotes as a means of inspiring their employees and coworkers and of keeping morale at a positive and productive level. Motivational quotes can provide an "uplifting push" and can lead to improved collegial relationships and better overall performance.

In conclusion, the influence of motivational quotes on people can be immense. Through the use of inspiring words, individuals can gain confidence and direction, leading to self-reflection and personal growth. Moreover, businesses can use motivational quotes to motivate and inspire their employees and co-workers, ultimately leading to more positive vibes and better performances. Motivational quotes are a perfect example of the power of words. Used to its fullest potential, it can have a leading and lasting effect on people.

CHAPTER FIVE

SEVEN TYPES OF MOTIVATION AND ITS IMPACT ON PEOPLE

Motivation is an important factor in determining how successful a person is in life. It can be seen as the drive or passion to reach a certain goal or perform a certain task. It is often the difference between success and failure, so it is important to understand the different types of motivation and how they can impact people.

First, there is intrinsic motivation. This type of motivation is internal and comes from the individual's own internal drive, desires, and interests. People with intrinsic motivation can be seen as self-motivated and are usually driven to perform even without external rewards. It is an important part of overall life satisfaction and can be an effective way to achieve goals.

Second, there is extrinsic motivation. This type of motivation is external and involves incentives, rewards, and punishments to drive behavior. Such rewards can provide a sense of accomplishment, boost morale, and give a person a sense of purpose. However, it can also be negative, creating feelings of fear or anxiety if the reward is threatened.

Third, there is social motivation. This involves other people, including friends, family, and peers. It is often used in peer pressure motivation and can be used both positively and negatively. Positive social motivation can be an effective way of achieving goals, whereas negative social motivation such as peer pressure can lead to opposing behaviors.

Fourth, there is achievement motivation. This is when an individual is driven to reach a certain level of success or status. This motivation type is often associated with success in different domains, such as education, sports, and the workplace. It is a driving force for high performance and thus, is a key factor in success.

Fifth, there is goal motivation. This is when an individual has set a certain goal and is highly motivated to reach it. It involves setting goals, obtaining the required resources, and taking the necessary steps towards reaching the goal. It is often a key factor in success and is important in many areas of life.

Sixth, there is identity motivation. This type of motivation involves developing a personal identity or sense of self. It is often driven by values, beliefs, and experiences, and is a key part of forming an individual's identity. It can be an important factor in achieving success and provides a foundation on which to build upon.

Finally, there is pleasure motivation. This is when an

individual seeks out activities that bring pleasure or satisfaction. It is often based on activities that are enjoyable or interesting, such as hobbies, sports, or even watching television. This type of motivation can be a great way to relax and refresh our minds, but can also lead to overindulgence.

In conclusion, motivation is a key factor in personal success and achievement. There are seven main types of motivation: intrinsic, extrinsic, social motivation, achievement, goal, identity, and pleasure. Each of these types of motivation has the potential to drive enthusiasm among people.

CHAPTER SIX

THE VITAL IMPORTANCE AND BENEFITS OF MOTIVATION

Motivation is one of the most important aspects of success in any field of endeavour. It is through motivation that individuals come to understand goals, and gain the confidence and drive to achieve them. The importance of motivation is essential in the attainment of any level of success, and understanding the benefits of motivation can lead to better applications and higher levels of success.

The first step in understanding motivation is to understand the concept of purpose. Having a purpose in life creates a sense of identity and provides an efficient direction in which to focus one's energies. Without purpose, energy is scattered, leading to a lack of focus and an inability to stay on track for long periods of time. In order to fo stay on track and reach one's goals, having a purpose is of the utmost importance.

Another important aspect of motivation is goal-setting. By creating measurable goals that are attainable, individuals can set targets to work towards and measure their progress towards those targets. This aids in motivation by providing tangible results that can motivate an individual to continue striving for their goals. Additionally, breaking down a large goal into smaller, attainable tasks can help an individual focus their efforts on each task one at a time.

Additionally, positive evaluation is essential in providing motivation. By evaluating oneself regularly and focusing on one's strengths and successes, an individual can be better motivated to continue striving towards a goal. By recognizing successes and failures, an individual can be better prepared to identify potential areas of improvement.

Finally, focus is important for staying motivated. By focusing on the present and on tasks that are realistically achievable, an individual can maintain a higher level of focus and improve their chances of success. Additionally, focus on the end goal and micro-goals along the way can help an individual stay motivated to keep striving towards success.

Motivation is an essential element of any successful endeavor. Having a purpose, setting measurable goals, maintaining a positive attitude, and focusing on the present are all vitally important in the achievement of any goal. By understanding the importance and benefits of motivation, an individual can be better prepared to attain success in any field of endeavor.

CHAPTER SEVEN

THREE DEFINITIONS AND DIMENSIONS OF MOTIVATION

Motivation is an essential part of an individual's life in achieving success in their personal, academic and professional endeavours. It is defined as the inner drive or enthusiasm to pursue a goal, either in the short or long term. Motivation can come from both internal and external sources, and when combined can lead to remarkable outcomes. In this essay, we will explore three definitions and dimensions of motivation.

The first definition of motivation is that of a psychological concept. According to this definition, motivation is made up of a combination of a person's desires and needs, values, aspirations and fears. It is shaped by the person's experiences and goals and results in certain psychological and physiological changes. These changes include a heightened state of arousal, increased mental focus and drive, increased physical stamina and increased emotive states. The different types of motivational behaviours are goal setting, self-efficacy and self-regulation.

The second definition of motivation is one related to an individual's performance. According to this definition, motivation is when individuals strive to improve their skills and abilities to higher levels of performance in order to gain greater levels of satisfaction. This definition focuses on the specific goals and behaviours that support the goal. It emphasizes the overall satisfaction and happiness with the goal achieved. Examples of such goals could include completing a degree, learning a new language or developing leadership skills.

The third definition of motivation is one related to the social sciences. This definition posits that motivation involves both personal and environmental factors. It is a dynamic process in which the individual's personalities, abilities, emotions and beliefs interact with the social context. It requires an understanding of both personal and environmental motives and their complex relationship. The dimensions of motivation in this definition include needs, motives, incentives, rewards and motivations.

In conclusion, it is clear that motivation is a multi-faceted concept. It is defined in three distinct ways: as a psychological concept, as a performance related concept, and as a social science concept. Each definition has its own unique set of dimensions related to it, and when taken together, they allow for a better understanding of this complex concept. Understanding motivation, how it works, and how it influences our behaviors is essential in developing healthy habits and achieving success.

CHAPTER EIGHT

SEVEN MOST EFFECTIVE MOTIVATIONAL QUOTES

Motivational quotes can be a powerful tool to help people find inspiration, achieve success, and overcome obstacles. Every individual has a need for motivation in order to succeed, and it is these quotes that can often provide the spark needed to take action and move forward. Here are twenty of the most effective motivational quotes that can help drive success and define success for each and every person.

The first quote comes from the Dalai Lama: "Remember that not getting what you want is sometimes a wonderful stroke of luck." Life is full of surprises and not always the ones we may prefer, but the outcome of these experiences can be the catalyst for growth and self-discovery. This quote is a reminder to stay optimistic and open minded to the possibilities of both positive and negative events.

The second quote is from Winston Churchill: "Success is not final, failure is not fatal: it is the courage to continue that counts." Too often, we focus on our failures and mistakes, and these can or block us from taking steps towards our goals. This quote encourages us to stay steadfast and courageous, while recognizing that these failures should not define success.

The third quote is from Aristotle: "We are what we repeatedly do. Excellence, then, is not an act, but a habit." When striving for greatness, it is important to recognize that success comes from dedication and hard work, not from a single moment. This quote underscores the importance of forming good habits that can produce long-term results.

The fourth quote is from Nelson Mandela: "Action without vision is only passing time, vision without action is merely day dreaming, but vision with action can change the world." Insights and ideas can have immense power when coupled with action, and this quote reminds us to take practical steps to bring our dreams and goals to life.

The fifth quote is from Mark Twain: "The secret of getting ahead is getting started." It often takes lots of courage to make the first step towards a goal. This quote emphasizes that great things come from taking action, no matter how intimidating it may seem.

The sixth quote comes from Confucius: "It does not matter how slowly you go as long as you do not stop." There are times that the journey towards success can be long and difficult, and this can often lead to feelings of despair and discouragement. This quote is a powerful reminder to stay dedicated and focused.

The seventh quote comes from Tony Robbins: "The path to success is to take massive, determined action." Commitment and action are two of the most important steps to success, and this quote serves as a call to action and a reminder to stay focused.

Dalai Lama

Winston Churchill

Aristotle

Nelson Mandela

Mark Twain

Confucius

Tony Robbins

MOST EFFECTIVE SEVEN MOTIVATIONAL QUOTES FOR NEW GENERATION

EFFECTIVE MOTIVATION FOR NEW GENERATION

Motivation is a key factor in enabling individuals to reach their goals and live a fulfilling life. To that end, motivational quotes often provide a useful and powerful tool in prompting us to take action and stay focused. With that in mind, here are seven inspiring and uplifting quotes which have made a profound impact on me.

The first quote I recall really resonating with me has been around for centuries: "If you want something you've never had, you have to do something you've never done." It reminds me of the power of taking risks and pushing our boundaries to make progress in life. When we stick within a comfort zone, it is difficult to make progress and grow. We must venture into the unknown and push our limits, in order to move forward.

The second quote I find particularly motivating is, "Don't let yesterday take up too much of today." Though there is value in learning from the past, it is much more powerful to focus on the present and take action in the here-and-now. By living in the 'now', the energy and enthusiasm to create a better future is much greater.

The third quote is one that can benefit all areas of life, "People who say it cannot be done should not interrupt those who are doing it." I find it particularly relevant to entrepreneurship, where a true innovator is often disregarded at first but ultimately successful. People will always say it can't be done. However, the person who has identified a need and found an innovative solution may ultimately prove them wrong.

The fourth quote is "The only way out is through." This reminds me that there is no shortcut or quick way around obstacles, and obstacles are to be expected in any journey. The only way to find success is to keep pushing forward and confront the challenge head-on.

The fifth quote is one of my favorites, "Go the extra mile, it's never crowded." This speaks to the power of putting in more effort than expected and going the extra mile. Too often, people are content to do the minimum effort, but only those willing to put in extra time and effort will realize their potential.

The sixth quote I often reflect upon is "It's not going to be easy but it's going to be worth it." This quote serves as an important reminder to keep pressing forward even when the going gets tough. No matter how difficult the challenge, the right attitude and grit will be rewarded in the long run.

Finally, the last quote I find particularly inspiring is "Success isn't always about greatness, it's about consistency." It's often easier to see the 'big wins', but behind every great success is a lot of hard work and patience are there.

CHAPTER ELEVEN

HOW MOTIVATION HELP YOU HIT YOUR GOALS

Motivation is a key factor in accomplishing goals. People who are able to stay motivated to pursue their goals often experience greater success than those who lack the drive and determination to push through the challenging aspects of any task. Motivation comes in many forms, and understanding the different types of motivation can help you better understand how to use each type to its fullest potential to hit your goals.

First, internal motivation drives a person to accomplish goals in order to achieve satisfaction and fulfilment, using their own level of self-determination. This type of motivation is often powerful and sustainable, since it comes directly from within and offers the necessary emotional push to move forward in a goal-directed manner. Making defined goals, setting rewards and timelines, and monitoring progress can all help to develop and maintain internal motivation, allowing you to stay determined and consistent throughout the process of reaching your goals.

Second, external motivation is often used to achieve goals by using external sources. This type of motivation could include external motivation sources such as acceptance, praise, rewards, or tangible benefits. External motivation is often short-term, as relying on external sources for motivation can easily lose its effect or become a substitute for any internal motivation a person may already possess.

Finally, intrinsic motivation is driven by the desire to do something for its inherent value or reward. It often arises from an individual's internal sense of enjoyment or appreciation of their task and can be incredibly powerful in reinforcing the goal-reaching process. Finding ways to tap into intrinsic motivation can be a great way to stay motivated throughout the goal-reaching process. This type of motivation is often more authentic and rewarding because it comes from within the individual.

Ultimately, motivation is uniquely personal and understanding different types of motivation can help you to find and sustain the drive necessary to meet your goals. Working to combine both internal and external sources of motivation as well as identifying intrinsic motivators can help ensure that you are on the right track to meeting your goals quickly and efficiently. With the proper motivation, hard work and dedication, you can hit your goals and reach success.

CHAPTER TWELVE

FIVE MOST MOTIVATIONAL PERSONALITIES AND THEIR ATTITUDE

Motivation has a powerful effect on our lives, making us want to do things more quickly and efficiently. People with a high level of motivation achieve their goals better and are able to motivate others in their lives. Throughout history, there have been many personalities that have had an impact on today's society because of their motivational stories. From high-profile business moguls to influential political leaders, these are five of the most inspirational and motivational personalities of all time.

ELON MUSK

Elon Musk is a business magnate, engineer, and inventor who is the founder, CEO, and chief designer of both SpaceX and Tesla Motors. Musk is a leader in the innovation age, pushing boundaries and unleashing the power of technology. He is not afraid to take risks and he has an amazing attitude of never giving up. His willingness to fail in order to learn and grow has been a key for his success. He is an eternal optimist who propels himself and others towards success by never stopping trying.

NELSON MANDELA

Nelson Mandela is a South African statesman and activist who served as the first president of his country after the fall of apartheid. He is well-known for his activism and championing of freedom and justice. He endured a long period of personal struggle and imprisonment, but his optimism never wavered. Mandela taught the world to never give up and always stand up for what is right, no matter how difficult the task may be. He faced some of the most challenging times of his life with grace and dignity, proving that anything is possible if you stay true to your beliefs.

OPRAH WINFREY

Oprah Winfrey is an American media mogul, talk show host, producer, and philanthropist. Winfrey is one of the most successful entrepreneurs of all time, and she has changed the lives of countless people through her unwavering optimism and ability to inspire. Winfrey has faced difficult times in her life, but she believes in the power of resilience and never gives up in the face of adversity. This attitude has enabled her to reinvent herself time and time again and remain at the top.

DWAYNE JOHNSON

Dwayne Johnson is an American actor, producer, and former professional wrestler. Johnson is known for his dynamic and outgoing personality, and his relentless pursuit of success and excellence. His motto, "it's not about how hard you hit, it's about how hard you can get hit and keep getting back up" has been adopted by many. He's a prime example of how to stay positive, motivated, and optimistic even in the toughest of times.

MALALA YOUSAFZAI

Malala Yousafzai is a Pakistani activist for female education and a Nobel Prize laureate. At 15 years old, she was the youngest person to ever receive the Nobel Prize. Yousafzai is an example of how determination and the courage to stand up for what is right can make a difference. She has shown the world that no matter how difficult the odds may be, with confidence and strength.

CHAPTER THIRTEEN

MOTIVATION – THEORIES & EXAMPLES

Motivation is a powerful force that can drive individuals to accomplish remarkable feats and generate positive changes in their lives. It is something that can be learned, cultivated, and improved upon. To understand motivation, it is important to be familiar with different motivational theories, examples, their impacts, and the importance of motivation in everyday life.

One of the first and most popular theories of motivation is the Self-Determination Theory. This theory suggests that all individuals have a need to be autonomous, competent, and connected to others; the satisfaction of these needs is what motivates people and enables them to gain psychological well-being. An example of this is when a person is given an important task at work. They feel competent to complete the task, they know that they have the autonomy to complete it in their own way, and they will also receive recognition from their coworkers for completing it. All of these factors contribute to the motivation to complete the task.

Another popular motivational theory is Herzberg's Two-Factor Theory. This theory states that motivation has two components: hygiene factors and motivators. Hygiene factors include things that can cause dissatisfaction if absent, such as fair wages, job security, and decent working conditions. Motivators, by contrast, are elements that create job satisfaction, such as recognition, achievement, and responsibility. An example of this is when a worker is motivated by the possibility of a promotion. The hygiene factor of fair wages and job security might not be enough to motivate the worker, but the possibility of achievement and recognition could be strong motivators.

The impact of motivational theories can be affected by the individual's psychological makeup. For instance, a person who is naturally pessimistic or has low self-esteem might find it difficult to tap into the motivators in a given situation. Similarly, someone who is naturally optimistic might find it easy to tap into their motivation. Despite these differences in individuals, motivational theories can still be effective in encouraging people to reach their goals.

Finally, the importance of motivation should not be underestimated. Having a strong sense of motivation can lead to enhanced performance, increased job satisfaction, better work-life balance, and stronger interpersonal relationships. Additionally, it can help individuals to stay focused, make decisions more quickly, and take on challenges that they might otherwise avoid. All of these factors combine to make motivation an invaluable tool for achieving goals and leading a happy and successful life.

• 46 •

In conclusion, motivation is a complex phenomenon that has been studied and analyzed for decades. Understanding motivational theories, examples, impacts, and importance is essential for helping individuals to achieve their goals and achieve success. As with all things, motivation requires practice and dedication, but the rewards are well worth the effort.

MOTIVATION THROUGH ART

Motivational art can be a powerful expression of hope, resilience and courage. It has the potential to provide a message of comfort and encouragement to individuals who may be feeling discouraged, disheartened and even hopeless. Digital art plays an important role in conveying the uplifting appeal of this form of art, particularly in its ability to easily reach a wide audience and provide a medium for creative expression.

Motivational digital art is often created with simple yet vibrant colors, textures and shapes to evoke a sense of inspiration and positivity. Oftentimes, these art pieces feature uplifting words or phrases, such as "Never give up" or "You can do it." By viewing these images, a person can be reminded not to lose sight of the possibility of a brighter tomorrow, even if their current struggles seem insurmountable. Moreover, the artist's creativity and individuality can be seen in each work, providing a unique form of motivation tailored to the individual.

In addition to providing a source of inspiration and hope, motivational digital art can also be a form of self-expression. The artist may create a piece based on personal experience and lessons they have learned, such as the importance of enjoying the present moment, striving to overcome adversity, or understanding that failure is an unavoidable part of life. By creating work based on these ideas, the artist can serve as a role model, demonstrating to those who are facing setbacks that it is possible to move forward with optimism and confidence.

At the same time, digital art can create a community of individuals who have the same goals and values, providing a sense of support and connection during times of disappointment. Through social media platforms and forums, artists with similar objectives can come together to provide advice, ideas and motivation to one another. By providing constructive feedback, members of this community can create a positive atmosphere where individuals can contribute to and benefit from the collective wisdom of others.

In conclusion, motivational digital art can be a powerful source of encouragement for people facing disappointment. Through a combination of creative expression, inspirational messages and a strong sense of community, this type of art has the potential to lift individuals out of despair and ensure that hope remains alive even in the darkest of times.

CHAPTER FIFTEEN

MOTIVATIONAL THERAPY

Motivational therapy, also known as mindfulness-based cognitive therapy, is becoming a popular therapeutic modality with individuals seeking to develop strategies to help them manage their psychology and emotions. This type of therapy uses scientific and practical strategies to assist people in exploring their capabilities and potential, and to make constructive changes in their life. It is especially helpful for those who are feeling despondent or discouraged and need a positive pathway forward.

Motivational therapy can provide individuals with the guidance and support they need to build resilience and to make tangible and effective changes in their lives. It is beneficial in helping individuals see beyond their current life difficulties and discover the potential they have to live a fulfilling life. Motivational therapy seeks to motivate an individual to move out of their comfort zone and to become a better version of themselves.

The aim of motivational therapy is to empower individuals to take control of their lives; to explore goals and develop healthy objectives. Therapists bring a feeling of hope and encouragement to the individual, acknowledging their current struggles but believing in their potential to overcome them. The therapist's approach emphasizes personal growth and incorporates various strategies to equip the individual with the necessary resources to work on personal development. This model of therapy focuses on the individual's strengths, capability of making positive changes to their life, and actively encourages and motivates them to embrace growth and self-realization.

Motivational therapy seeks to provide individuals with a more positive outlook on life, to assist them with developing coping strategies and to break free of barriers to ensure they can benefit from a multidimensional view of life. It seeks to guide people towards a more optimistic attitude and to appreciate the small successes each day. This approach allows a person to gain an awareness of their own capabilities and discover they have access to an internal drive and motivation to improve their life.

Motivational therapy can provide many benefits in helping people who are feeling discouraged and despondent. It seeks to provide realistic solutions and help the individual build a fulfilling life for themselves. It is designed to support individuals in setting realistic achievable goals and developing strategies to achieve them. It is effective in helping people to gain control of their life and take responsibility for their actions. Ultimately, it seeks to create an environment that allows individuals realize and believe in their potential.

CHAPTER SIXTEEN

INSPIRATIONAL PEOPLE & THEIR ATTITUDE

An inspirational person is someone who recognises their own strengths and limitations as well as the abilities of others, possesses a creative and open mind, and embraces change and challenges. Inspirational people have an uncompromising attitude and a passionate commitment to their personal mission. They draw on both their successes and failures, seeking to use them as opportunities for growth and development.

The attitude of inspirational people is often described as optimistic and hopeful. They know that making an effort to motivate, lead, and positively communicate with others can make a great difference in how successful a team or an organization is as a whole. They focus on the collective effort and encourage people to work together to reach a common goal. They are confident in their abilities and trust that their efforts will help them achieve their desired outcome.

The teaching techniques used by inspirational people vary depending on the context. When teaching through example, they emphasize the value of hard work, passion, and commitment. They strive to bring out the best in others and recognize their individual strengths and weaknesses. They also incorporate their own experiences and achievements as a way to show their students how to apply concepts and principles in their daily lives.

Inspirational people use storytelling as a way to educate and motivate their students. They use dramatic retellings to illustrate a point, create an emotional connection between themselves and the students, and more effectively captivate their attention. By using stories that involve real-life people and situations, students are able to gain insight into difficult concepts, as well as gain an appreciation for the subject matter.

In order to foster an environment of mutual respect, inspirational people listen to the opinions of their students, taking time to get to know their individual operating styles and preferences. They go the extra mile to ensure their students have all the resources they need in order to learn the material and ask thought-provoking questions to encourage critical thinking. They also emphasize the importance of collaboration and inclusiveness.

In summary, inspirational people bring out the best in others by setting a good example, determinedly pursuing personal and organizational goals, and utilizing creative teaching techniques to facilitate learning. They inspire others through their optimism, efforts, and trust in the abilities of their students. Ultimately, they embody an attitude of hope, personal commitment, and confidence that encourages others to excel.

CHAPTER SEVENTEEN

ROUTINE OF MOTIVATIONAL PEOPLE

Motivational people are the backbone of many organizations and individual lives. They come in different forms, from celebrities to athletes to entrepreneurs, but they are all tied together by a common template: the routine of motivational people. This routine often consists of words, style, and walk, and is a method to instill a sense of purpose and drive into those around them.

The first element of the motivational routine is often rooted in words. These words can vary greatly depending on who is speaking. For example, celebrities often use a mixture of amusing quips and emotionally-charged phrases to inspire their fans. On the other hand, athletes use empowering mantras to keep them focused on the long-term goals that the audience benefits from. And entrepreneurs often use simple, direct directives to provide the necessary guidance and instructions to those they are influencing. Regardless of the words, their purpose is to deliver a positive, uplifting message to their audience.

The second element of the motivational routine is often a particular style. Motivational people tend to use a combination of gestures and body language to reinforce their words. They might point to emphasize key points, use powerful hand gestures to demonstrate their enthusiasm, or wave away their detractors. Motivational people also tend to have a certain level of charisma that radiates from their body language. They often have a kind of coolness and easy confidence that sets them apart from the rest of the crowd.

The third element of the motivational routine is their walk. Motivational people tend to have a purposeful, energetic walk that can signal to their audience that there is work to be done. They often lead the charge and signal to those around them to follow their lead. They might quicken their pace to convey urgency, or merely raise their shoulders and tilt their head forward to signal a need to stay focused.

At the end of the day, it is the routine of motivational people that helps them to inspire and motivate their audience. From the words they choose, to the style they embody, to the walk they take, their routine is an instrumental part of their journey. It sets the tone, and is ultimately what drives motivation in those around them.

CHAPTER EIGHTEEN

HOW SUCCESSFUL PEOPLE MOTIVATE OTHERS BY THEIR ACTIONS

Successful people are role models for the younger generation, inspiring others to work towards achieving a higher standard of achievement. They encourage and empower those around them to follow their footsteps and reap the rewards of working hard. The most successful people can motivate others by their actions by providing examples of the dedication and perseverance it takes to reach a certain level.

The most successful people motivate others by embodying the hard work they needed to put in to achieve their goals. Successful people know that hard work and motivation are necessary components of success, and so they set an example by showing others what it takes. For example, successful people put in long hours of work, stay focused on their goals, and persist in the face of failure. These qualities can provide others with the encouragement and ambition to work towards achieving their own goals.

Moreover, successful people are often great teachers and communicators. They use their experience to explain why hard work is necessary and how it can lead to rewards. They can provide tangible advice and mentorship so that others can take the necessary steps to make their dreams come true. In addition to providing concrete examples of success, successful people also inspire others with their stories of how they overcame obstacles and figured out strategies for achieving their goals. Such stories of overcoming adversity and staying resolute can serve to inspire others and enable them to take the necessary steps to reach their own success.

Overall, successful people can motivate others by their actions by exhibiting dedication and perseverance, embodying the work ethic necessary for success, providing mentorship, and inspiring others with their stories. These qualities, when exhibited by successful people, can provide motivating examples and encouragement for those who yearn to achieve the same level of success. By providing tangible advice and tangible examples of success, successful people can, in turn, help others to reach their goals.

CHAPTER NINETEEN

MOST INSPIRING 10 MOTIVATIONAL BOOKS

In today's world, motivation has become an important factor in developing success. Everyone needs a push to stay motivated and make a change that can be positive for everyone. This is where motivational books come into play. It is a collection of literature designed to help readers become more confident and inspired to take on their goals. In this essay, I will discuss the most inspiring and motivational books and the content each one offers.

The first book that is highly recommended as a motivational book is 'Awaken the Giant Within' by Anthony Robbins. This book has been called a 'handbook for personal and business transformation', and it is a powerful program that encourages readers to take control of their lives and think positively. This book will help people learn how to create a powerful internal drive, kick-start their self-motivation and gain control over the subconscious mind.

'The Power of Positive Thinking' by Norman Vincent Peale has been a long-time favourite around the world. This book contains a powerful message of self-improvement and encourages readers to have faith in themselves and focus on the best in life. Peale's message is simple, but effective; by changing the way we think, we can drastically change our lives for the better.

Another popular motivational book is 'The 7 Habits of Highly Effective People' by Stephen Covey. This book is all about the importance of creating a personal philosophy and developing the necessary habits to become successful. Specifically, this book discusses the need for creating proactive habits that allow readers to be more effective and make better decisions.

The next book is 'The Power of Now' by Eckhart Tolle. This one is focused on gaining insight and understanding into the present moment. Tolle states that the key to living a meaningful life is focusing on the present and learning how to accept yourself and the world around you.

'The 48 Laws of Power' by Robert Greene is an excellent book for anyone looking to gain a better understanding of the power dynamics in relationships and achieve success in life. This book goes beyond the traditional books on motivation and would be an invaluable source of knowledge to anyone looking to understand the true nature of power.

'The Magic of Thinking Big' by David Schwartz is also a great motivational book. This one focuses on the importance of having a big vision and the power of goal setting. This book encourages readers to have faith in themselves and their own abilities and constantly push themselves to think bigger and more positively.

'Feel the Fear and Do It Anyway' by Susan Jeffers is focused on conquering our fears and tackling any obstacle that may come our way. Jeffers encourages readers to never shrink away from their fears, but rather confront them head on and turn them into a source of strength and motivation.

CHAPTER TWENTY

MOST INSPIRING MOTIVATIONAL PERSON OF AMERICA

Frederick Douglass is an iconic figure, who is often considered to be "America's most inspiring motivational person." In the 19th century, Douglass wrote numerous books and other works, inspiring others to pursue justice and freedom in the United States, particularly from the bonds of slavery.

Douglass was born in February 1818, in Talbot County, Maryland. His mother was a black slave who died shortly after he was born, and his father was a white man whom he never met. At the age of seven, Douglass was sent to live with the slaveholder's family, although he was frequently loaned out to work as a labourer on nearby farms.

In 1838, Douglass escaped from slavery and moved north to Pennsylvania. Having little formal education while a slave, but having remarkable eagerness to learn, Douglass managed to teach himself and eventually moved to New Bedford, Massachusetts. Here, he married and obtained a career as a advocate of the antislavery cause.

Douglass' first published works were written largely in part due to his friend and mentor William Lloyd Garrison, who believed that the civil war could be won through "moral suasion". Having written numerous pamphlets and letters to increase Northern support for the antislavery cause, Douglass growing recognition and notoriety as an outstanding public speaker also enabled him to draw large crowds.

In addition to these activities, Douglass authored three autobiographies, My Bondage and My Freedom (1855), Life and Times of Frederick Douglass (1881) and The Life of Frederick Douglass (1892). Through these works Douglass inspired the American public to realize the wrongs of slavery and to seek a better life for blacks in the United States. His works explored the hardships and revelations he faced during his time as a slave, offering hope and strength through understanding.

As an author and public speaker, Douglass also created hope and strength in his audiences by imploring them to use their energy and voices to create a better world. Through his works, Douglass presented a masterful ability to reach and move his audiences, to make complex concepts more accessible, to open conversations, and to ultimately empower those around him.

The works of Frederick Douglass is continuously sought out by many to this day. His books are a testament of the power of self-discovery, showing readers that no matter the obstacles or hardships, one has the power to make a difference. In this way, many believe that Douglass should be regarded as America's most inspiring motivational person. His books are still widely read and continue to amaze, guide and inspire countless of people.

CHAPTER TWENTY-ONE

MOTIVATIONAL SPEECH THAT CHANGES THE WORLD

The speech that changed the world was given by Nelson Mandela in his inauguration address, delivered on May 10th, 1994 in Pretoria, South Africa as his nation's first black President. In this landmark speech, Mandela spoke with a unifying and inspirational force about his belief in peace and reconciliation amidst a nation divided by the legacy of apartheid.

As Mandela opened his address, he reminded the nation of its long history of racial oppression and declared change necessary for the nation to thrive. He said, "Never, never, and never again shall it be that this beautiful land will again experience the oppression of one by another." As he spoke to the previous rulers of South Africa, he also reminded them that enemies of yesterday should be partners of today, and none can place themselves above others. In addition, he declared it would take hard work and devotion to build a bridge of understanding, rather than a wall of divide. This bridge of understanding, he warned, could not be built on the foundation of those unwilling to forgive.

To bring unity to the fractured nation, Mandela called for new economic and political programs that would begin the healing process and unite all South Africans. He declared that education and health care should be made available to all, and that government would strive to replace poverty with hope and prosperity. Additionally, he proclaimed that no citizen should be treated differently based on their background or race. This, Mandela declared, should be a fundamental right of all South Africans.

Prior to Mandela's speech, South African citizens had long been separated by hatred and prejudice. With his passionate words, Mandela emerged as a powerful leader, speaking of peace, acceptance and equality. These core values resonated deeply with South Africa's citizens, inspiring a sense of shared purpose and responsibility to build a better country.

In his address, Mandela made an appeal for courage, calling people to face fears and kindness and earn the freedom of the nation. His power of words was infectious, igniting a spirit of change and progress in South Africa and inspiring people around the world. As he declared, "Let there be justice for all. Let there be peace for all. Let there be work, bread, water and salt for all."

As a result, Mandela's inauguration speech was a driving force of change, a vision of change, and a cornerstone for a peaceful nation. His wise words of hope and unity will continue to be remembered as a powerful speech that changed the world.

CHAPTER TWENTY-TWO

MOST EFFECTIVE MOTIVATIONAL QUOTES ONE BY ONE

Motivation is an integral part of our lives, helping us to stay focused, inspired and driven. Having the right motivational quotes can be a great way to stay motivated and help us to reach our goals. Here are some of the most popular and effective motivational quotes of all time.

First, there's the timeless quote by Henry Ford, "Whether you think you can or cannot, you're right." This posits the idea that our actions and thoughts are what shapes our reality. Whether we choose to believe we can do something or not, our attitude will always have a large impact on the outcome. It's a reminder to stay positive and motivated, focus on what we're capable of, and have the confidence to try new things.

Second is a quote by Rudy Ruettiger, "The only man who never make a mistake is the man who never does anything." This quote is a reminder that mistakes are unavoidable in life and to fear them less. It encourages us to take risks and pursue our dreams, no matter how impossible they may seem. It's a great quote to keep in mind anytime we are feeling scared to go after our goals.

Third, there's an inspirational quote by Mahatma Gandhi, "You must be the change you want to see in the world." This is one of the most important motivational quotes out there. It's a reminder that we are the ones responsible for making the world a better place; we can't simply rely on others to do it for us. It encourages us to take responsibility and be the change we wish to see in the world.

Fourth, a timeless quote from the movie The Shawshank Redemption, "Hope is a good thing, maybe the best of things, and no good thing ever dies." We all face difficult times, and this quote is a reminder that hope is never lost. It inspires us to stay strong no matter how dark the times are and keep faith that better days are ahead.

Finally, here's a quote from Dr. Seuss, "You're off to great places. Today is your day. Your mountain is waiting, so get on your way." This is one of the most encouraging and energizing motivational quotes out there. It's a reminder to stay focused on our goals and keep moving forward, no matter how tough the journey may be.

Motivational quotes can be a great source of positivity and encouragement. Keeping these quotes in mind can help to keep us focused and driven, helping us to stay motivated and reach our goals.

Contact

DR. JAGADEESH PILLAI

9839093003

myrichindia@gmail.com

facebook.com/drjagadeeshpillai

drjagadeeshpillai@youtube

www.JAGADEESHPILLAI.com